SNARKY CROSS-STITCH KIT

Publications International, Ltd.

Cover and interior art: Shiho Akaike and Kelsey Waitkus

Photography: Christopher Hiltz and Shutterstock.com

Louis Weber, CEO
Publications International, Ltd.
8140 Lehigh Avenue
Morton Grove, IL 60053

ISBN: 978-1-68022-538-9

Manufactured in China.

8 7 6 5 4 3 2 1

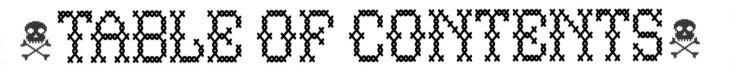

TABLE OF CONTENTS

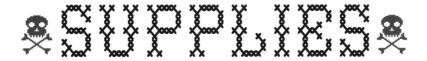

SUPPLIES

If you can read a chart and have a proclivity for criticism, you can do snarky cross-stitch. Here are some supplies you'll need aside from your attitude and design chart.

Fabrics

Most counted cross-stitch is done on Aida fabric or evenweave fabric. Aida fabric is woven in square blocks and evenweave is woven with single threads. On Aida fabric, a cross-stitch is worked over one square block. On evenweave fabric, a cross-stitch is worked "over two threads."

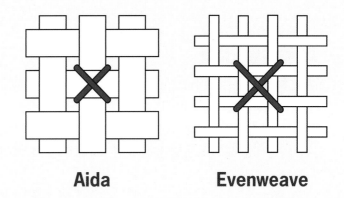

Aida   **Evenweave**

Aida

Aida fabric is perfect for beginners. Its precise, square-patterned weave creates visible holes that make Aida simple to use. Aida fabric is available in a variety of different counts, including 6, 8, 11, 14, 16, and 18. The most common is 14-count Aida. The count indicates how many squares there are per inch of fabric. For example, 14-count Aida has 14 squares per inch.

Evenweave

The term evenweave refers to fabric having the same number of threads per inch vertically and horizontally. The thread count for evenweave fabric indicates the number of threads per inch. For example, 22-count evenweave fabric has 22 horizontal threads and 22 vertical threads per inch. The greater the thread count per inch, the finer the fabric.

Other Materials

In addition to Aida and evenweave fabrics, a number of other materials can be used for cross-stitching. Plastic canvas, vinyl, perforated paper, perforated metal, and even baskets with a fairly even weave can be cross-stitched. You can also purchase ready-made items with panels of Aida cloth for cross-stitching.

Floss

Embroidery floss, or thread, is available in many forms and colors. You can buy it in your local craft store in skeins, hanks, spools, or balls. Most embroidery floss consists of six strands twisted together. The six-strand cotton embroidery floss is generally cut into 18-inch lengths for stitching. Use two of the six strands for cross-stitching on 14-count Aida. You will usually use one or two strands for backstitching. Refer to individual patterns for how many strands to use.

Needles

Most cross-stitching is done with a tapestry needle. Tapestry needles have blunt, rounded tips and long oval eyes. Needles come in various sizes. As a general rule, the smaller the needle size, the greater the length of the needle and eye. A size 24 needle is recommended for cross-stitching on 14-count Aida.

For French knots and backstitches, some people prefer a sharper, finer embroidery needle.

When incorporating beads into a design, a beading needle works best. Beading needles are long and thin enough to pass easily through the holes in the beads.

Needle Threaders

As the name suggests, needle threaders help you thread the embroidery floss through the eye of the needle.

To use a needle threader, slide the folded wire of the needle threader through the eye of the needle. Insert the floss through the folded wire loop of the needle threader. Draw the wire loop and floss back through the eye of the needle.

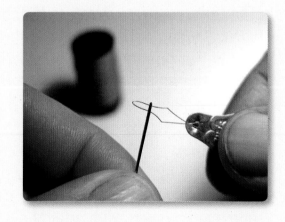

Embroidery Hoops

Embroidery hoops consist of two rings made of wood or plastic. They hold your fabric between the two rings so that your fabric is stretched out evenly while you stitch. You can use an embroidery hoop if you like, but it is not necessary for cross-stitching on Aida cloth. If you do use an embroidery hoop, be sure to remove it when not working on your piece, so that the creases will be easier to remove later.

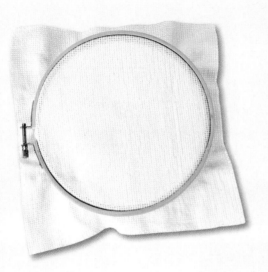

To use an embroidery hoop, first place the fabric over the smaller inner ring. Then place the larger outer ring over the fabric. Press until the bottom ring fits snugly inside the top ring. Gently tug the edges of the fabric until the fabric is taut. Tighten the screw.

Scissors

You will want a pair of small, sharp embroidery scissors for cutting embroidery floss. Use a pair of dressmaking shears to cut Aida fabric.

Thread Organizers

For projects with numerous floss colors, it helps to organize your threads. Before starting your project, you can organize your floss by color with a thread organizer. You can purchase a thread organizer at your local craft store or you can make your own. Punch holes for each floss color in a piece of cardboard or a stiff piece of paper. Label each hole with the floss shade number or pattern symbol for reference. Cut the floss into manageable lengths of about 18 inches. Fold in half and loop through separate holes in the thread organizer.

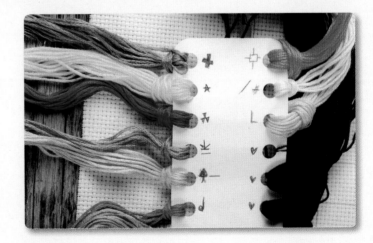

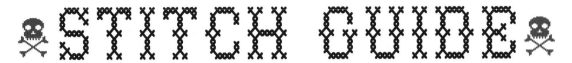
There are six basic stitches used in cross-stitch—cross-stitch, half stitch, quarter stitch, three-quarter stitch, backstitch, and French knot. Half stitches, quarter stitches, and three-quarter stitches are sometimes called fractional stitches. Fractional stitches and another stitch called the Smyrna stitch are more advanced.

Cross-Stitch (X)

There are two common cross-stitching methods. One method completes each individual cross-stitch before moving on to the next. The other method makes a row of half stitches and then returns, making the half stitches in the other direction to complete the stitches.

Making a Single Cross-Stitch

Step 1: Bring the needle from the back of the fabric through a hole to the front of the fabric. Make a diagonal stitch, bringing the needle up at 1 and down at 2.

Step 2: Bring the needle up at 3 and down at 4 to complete a single cross-stitch.

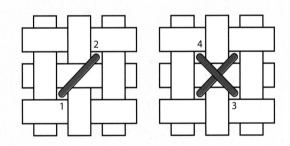

Making a Row of Cross-Stitches

Step 1: Bring the needle up from the back of the fabric at 1 and down at 2. Continue making a row of half stitches, bringing the needle up at 3, down at 4, up at 5, down at 6, and so on.

Step 2: Now make a row of half stitches in the opposite direction to complete the stitches. Bring the needle up at 7, down at 8, up at 9, down at 10, and so on until the row of cross-stitches is complete.

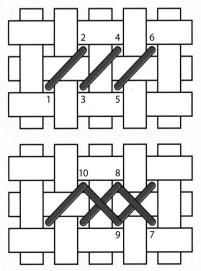

Vertical Cross-Stitch

Step 1: Make a column of half stitches, bringing the needle up at 1, down at 2, up at 3, down at 4, up at 5, and down at 6.

Step 2: Cross the stitches in the opposite direction, bringing the needle up at 7, down at 8, up at 9, down at 10, and so on.

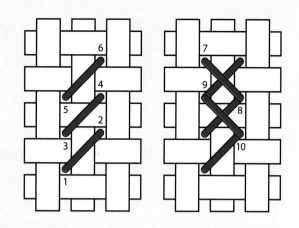

Backstitch (BS)

When backstitching, you pass the needle back down through the fabric at the same space as the previous backstitch. Bring the needle up at 1, down at 2, up at 3, down at 4, up at 5, down at 6, and so on.

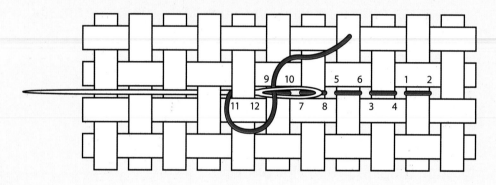

Half Stitch (1/2)

A half stitch is half of a full cross-stitch. Make a diagonal stitch, bringing the needle up at 1 and down at 2. To make a row of half stitches, bring the needle up at 3, down at 4, up at 5, down at 6, and so on.

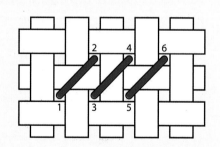

Quarter Stitch (1/4)

To make a quarter stitch, bring the needle up at 1. Then bring the needle down at 2, through the solid center of the square. Quarter stitches can be made in all directions.

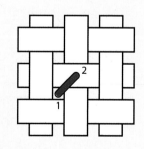

Three-Quarter Stitch (3/4)

Bring the needle up at 1 and down at 2. Bring the needle up at 3 and down through the center of the square at 4 to complete the three-quarter stitch. Three-quarter stitches can be made in all directions.

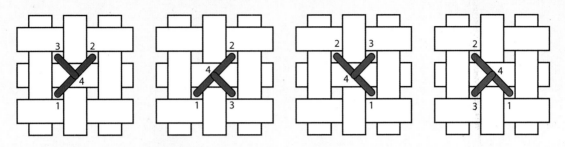

Smyrna Stitch (Spec)

Smyrna stitch is also called double cross-stitch.

Bring the needle up at 1, down at 2, up at 3, down at 4, up at 5, down at 6, up at 7, and down at 8 to complete the Smyrna stitch.

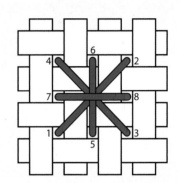

French Knot (FK)

Bring the needle up to the front. Wrap the floss around the needle (once for a small knot, more for a larger knot). Pull the floss end gently until the wrapped floss tightens around the needle. Holding the floss taut with one hand, insert the needle next to where you brought it up. Draw the needle and floss through to the back, holding the floss until it must be released.

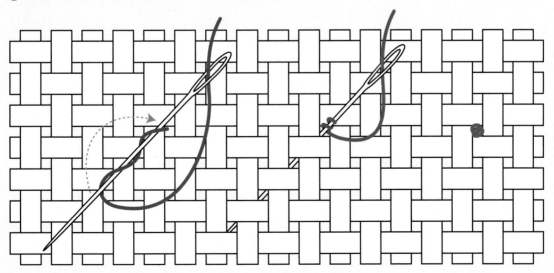

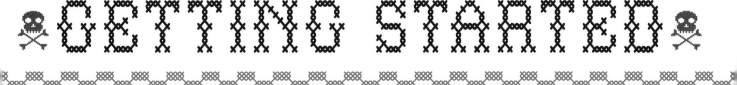

GETTING STARTED

Before embarking on any cross-stitch project, you'll need to select and prepare your materials.

Selecting Fabrics

The fabric in this kit is 14-count Aida, and most of the projects are worked on 14-count Aida cloth. Here are some things to keep in mind if selecting fabric for other projects:

- Aida is best for beginners. It's woven in blocks, giving the fabric obvious holes for the needle to go through.

- Quarter stitches and three-quarter stitches are harder to make on Aida because the needle goes through the middle of a square, which doesn't have a hole.

- Cross-stitches are worked over one square block with Aida fabric; on linen and other evenweaves, cross-stitches are generally worked "over two threads," so the needle enters alternating holes.

- Most evenweave fabrics are softer and less stiff than Aida.

- Each square on the chart represents one block of Aida cloth or two threads of evenweave fabric.

Selecting Needles

Different needles are designed for different jobs. When selecting a needle, consider the fabric and the job at hand. You will do most of your counted cross-stitch with a tapestry needle. Tapestry needles have a large eye to accommodate multiple strands of floss and a blunt tip that passes through holes in the fabric without tearing fibers. The size of your tapestry needle depends on your fabric. While tapestry needle sizes may vary slightly between manufacturers, use the table on the next page as a general guide.

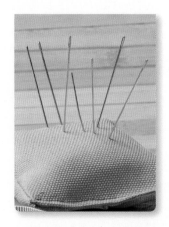

Needle size	Fabric
18	6-count Aida / 10-count evenweave
20	8-count Aida
22	11-count Aida / 22-25-27 count evenweave
24	14-count Aida / 28-count evenweave
26	16-count Aida / 32-count evenweave
28	18-count Aida / 36-55 count evenweave

Here are some other useful needles you can purchase:

Embroidery or crewel needles are thinner than tapestry needles and have a long eye and a sharp tip.

Chenille needles are thicker than embroidery needles and have a long eye and sharp tip.

Beading needles are long and very thin, used for stitching beads to fabric in cross-stitch designs because tapestry needles are too big.

Preparing Fabric

Many patterns will tell you how large a piece of fabric you will need to make the design. Allow some extra space for a border to protect yourself should you not get the design centered exactly. If the design will be framed or made into a pillow, add at least 3 inches on each of the sides. Cut fabric evenly along the vertical and horizontal threads to the desired size.

Locating the Center of Design and Fabric

Locating the center of your fabric is important so that you can center the design. Fold fabric lightly in half and then in half again to find the center. The center is where the folds intersect. You can locate the center of the design chart by following the arrows on the sides. You can also count up or over to another point on the chart and then count the corresponding number of squares on your cloth to find the same place.

Reading the Chart

A cross-stitch design chart, or pattern, is made up of small squares on a grid. The squares on the chart correspond to the squares on the fabric. Each stitch is represented by a symbol or line on the chart. Once you locate an item on the chart, find it in the key. The key tells you the color, stitch, and number of strands to use. Many charts have darker grid lines surrounding 10 x 10 sections to make it easier to count your stitches and keep your place. Blank squares on the chart indicate fabric squares to be left unstitched.

When cross-stitching on Aida, each square on the chart represents a square block on the fabric. When cross-stitching on evenweave fabric, each square on the chart represents two fabric threads.

GETTING READY TO STITCH

Separating Strands

Most embroidery floss, or thread, consists of six strands twisted together. The number of strands you will use depends on the fabric count. For 14-count Aida fabric, you will typically use two strands of floss for cross-stitches and one or two strands for backstitches. Most patterns will specify the number of strands to use.

Tip: To rejoin strands of floss, hold them together at one end and gently stroke them until smooth. Then twirl them together to recombine.

Threading the Needle

After you have separated the individual strands of floss, thread your tapestry needle with the required number of strands. Most cross-stitching on 14-count Aida is done with two strands.

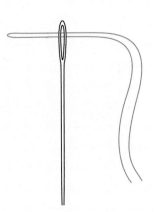

Tip: If stitching with two strands of floss, you can cut a length of floss twice as long as you would normally use and separate one strand rather than two. You can then fold the strand of floss in half and thread the needle with both ends.

STARTING TO STITCH

Select a floss color and stitch all of that color within an area. After you have separated the individual strands of floss, thread your tapestry needle with the required number of strands.

To start stitching, hold the end(s) of the floss behind the fabric until secured and covered over with a few stitches. This is sometimes called the "stitching over" method and is recommended for beginners. You may skip a few stitches to get from one area to another on the back of the fabric, but don't run floss behind an area that will not be stitched in the final piece because it will show through the fabric, particularly if the floss is a dark shade.

Stopping

To stop stitching, weave or run the floss under several stitches on the back side until secure. Clip the ends close to the work on the back. To resume stitching, rethread the needle and secure the new floss by weaving or running it under several stitches on the back side.

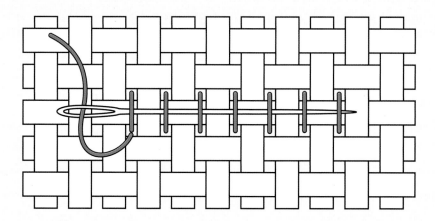

Loop Start

You can also anchor the floss to your fabric with a loop. This method only works when stitching with an even number of strands. If stitching with an even number of strands, start with half of the total number of strands you need (for stitching with two strands, use one; for four strands, use two) and cut double the length you need. Fold in half and thread through needle.

To start with a loop, bring the needle up from the back where you want your first stitch, leaving the looped end on the back side of the fabric. Make a half cross-stitch and bring the needle through the loop on the back side. Pull the floss until the loop is secure against the fabric.

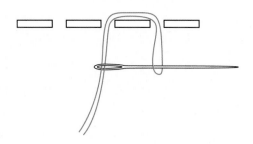

Waste Knot Start

A waste knot is another way to anchor your floss. To start, knot one end of the floss and pass your needle through the fabric, from front to back, about an inch from where your first cross-stitch will go. Bring your needle up from back to front at the starting point of your first cross-stitch. Stitch toward the knot, making sure your stitches cover the floss on the back. When you reach the knot, cut it from the front of the fabric and continue stitching.

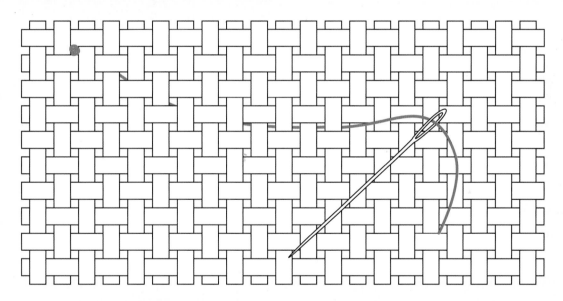

Stitching Tips

- Cross all stitches in the same direction. For horizontal rows, work the entire row of diagonal half stitches and then cross them coming back across the row.

- Start stitching in the center of the fabric and work out from there.

- Stitch with the darker colors first, then finish with the lighter colors.

- Avoid running floss across the back side of the fabric to jump to a new design area, especially with dark colors. It can show on the front. Only run floss across the back when the jump is short and the floss is a light color.

- For neat, uniform cross-stitches, keep your tension consistent throughout.

- Work all cross-stitches and fractional stitches first. Then work any backstitches. If French knots are used, work these last.

- Keeping your hands clean is the best way to keep your cross-stitch project clean.

Stitching with Beads

The same charts can be used for counted beading. Small colored beads are sewn to the fabric to create the design. Use a beading needle (a very fine needle with a sharp point) and sewing thread the same color as the fabric.

Bring the needle up from the back of the fabric to the front. Pass the needle through the hole in the bead. Make a diagonal stitch (half of a full cross-stitch), passing the needle from the front of the fabric to the back. You can either work from left to right or from right to left, but be sure all stitches go in the same direction so that the beads lie properly.

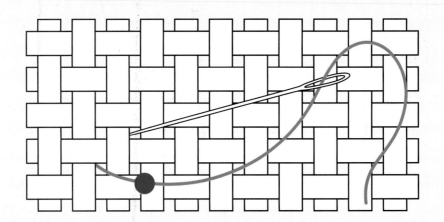

Caring for Fabric

Keeping your hands clean will go a long ways toward keeping your fabric clean. Should your fabric become soiled, wash it gently in cold water with a small amount of mild detergent or dishwashing liquid. DO NOT use Woolite, other specially for-mulated wool washes, strong detergents, or chlorine bleach. Rinse thoroughly with cold water and roll in a clean towel to remove excess water. Do not scrub, twist, or wring the fabric. Unroll while still damp and place face down between two tow-els. Press lightly with a warm iron.

I READ TO IGNORE YOU
☠ BOOKMARK ☠

Supplies:

- 14-count Aida cloth
- Tapestry needle
- 6-strand floss

Stitch this forthright bookmark with the 14-count Aida cloth and floss from the kit.

Design size:

104w x 30h stitches (7.4" x 2.1")

Instructions:

Following the general instructions on pages 09–10, stitch according to the chart. Squares in the chart that are only half filled use a half stitch.

Tip: There are a number of products you can purchase to help give your bookmark added strength and stability, including interfacing, fabric adhesive, and fusible bonding web. Fusible bonding web has a heat-activated adhesive that permanently glues the back of your bookmark to a piece of backing fabric without any sewing.

 Grey

 Bright Red

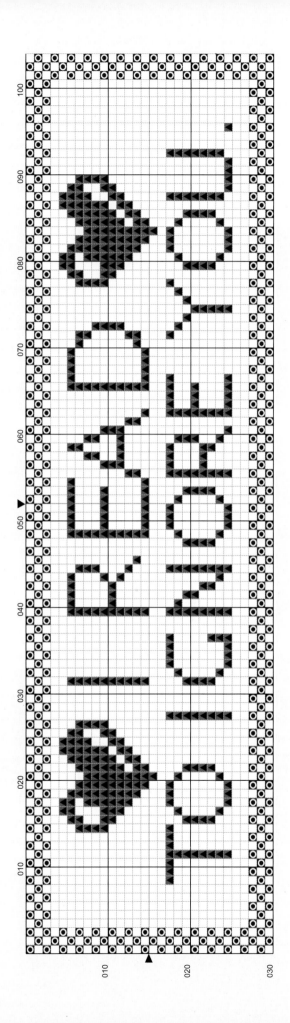

21

I AM THE ✠ BOOKMARK ✠

This antagonizing bookmark makes sure everyone knows who they're messing with.

Supplies:

- 14-count Aida cloth
- Tapestry needle
- 6-strand floss
- 7" x 2" piece of white felt (optional)
- Fusible bonding web (optional)

Design size:

104w x 30h stitches (7.4" x 2.1")

Instructions:

Following the general instructions on pages 09–10, stitch in 2 strands according to the chart.

Tip: Iron-on fusible bonding web allows you to permanently join fabric layers without sewing. Place a piece of fusible bonding web between the back of your bookmark and the felt piece. Following the manufacturer's directions, iron to bond the pieces of fabric.

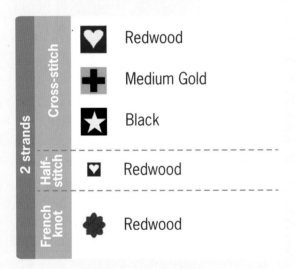

Cross-stitch	♥	Redwood
	✚	Medium Gold
	★	Black
Half-stitch	♥	Redwood
French knot	✿	Redwood

2 strands

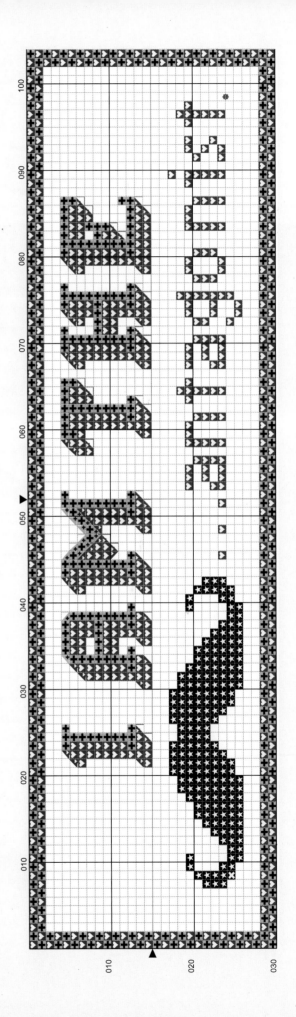

MY CRITICISM IS SHARPER THAN YOUR KNIFE
☠ BOOKMARK ☠

This self-defensive bookmark is sure to keep the hoodlums away.

Supplies:

- 14-count Aida-cloth
- Tapestry needle
- 6-strand floss

Design size:

102w x 28h stitches (7.3" x 2")

Instructions:

Following the general instructions on pages 09–10, stitch in 2 strands according to the chart.

		Cross-stitch
✚	Medium Gold	
◉	Grey	
▲	Bright Red	
◈	Dark Green	
▢	Light Green	
←	Medium Tan	

Back-stitch

— Grey

Half-stitch

◉	Grey
◈	Dark Green
←	Medium Tan
▲	Bright Red
✚	Medium Gold

French knot

✿ Grey

(2 strands)

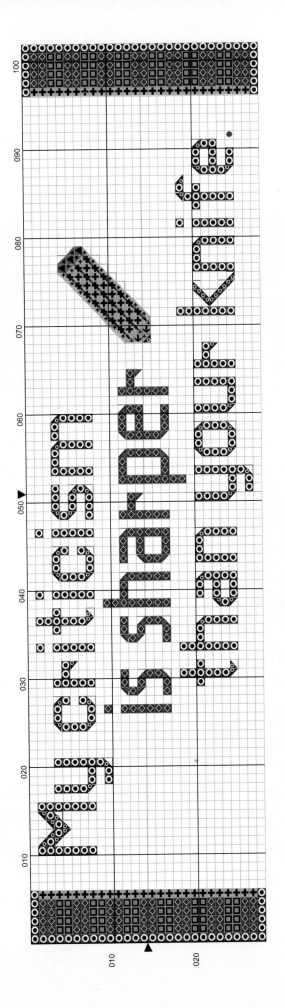

THE HERO DIES
☠ BOOKMARK ☠

Supplies:

- 14-count Aida cloth
- Tapestry needle
- 6-strand floss

Cross-stitch this bookmark to mark your place and give away the ending to your neighbor.

Design size:

102w x 28h stitches (7.3" x 2")

Instructions:

Following the general instructions on pages 09–10, stitch according to the chart. Squares in the chart that are only half filled use a half stitch. Allow about an extra half-inch of fabric beyond the stitched border on each side if you wish to fringe the edges.

Tip: After completing all cross-stitching, you can create fringed edges. Trim the Aida cloth, leaving some extra space around the sides of the bookmark. Gently pull loose strands of cloth around the edges up to the cross-stitched border without any sewing.

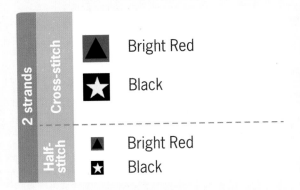

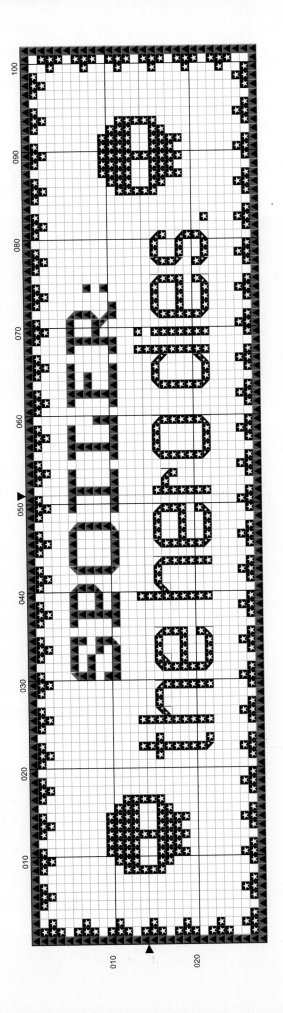

I CAN'T HEAR YOU, I'M READING ☠ BOOKMARK ☠

Supplies:
- 14-count Aida cloth
- Tapestry needle
- 6-strand floss

I can't hear you. I'm reading.

Cross-stitch this snarky bookmark for your favorite bookworm.

Design size:

104w x 30h stitches (7.4" x 2.1")

Instructions:

Following the general instructions on pages 09–10, cross-stitch in 2 strands according to the chart.

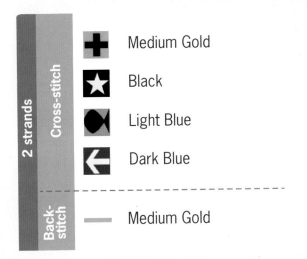

2 strands

Cross-stitch

Back-stitch

➕ Medium Gold

⭐ Black

🐟 Light Blue

⬅ Dark Blue

— Medium Gold

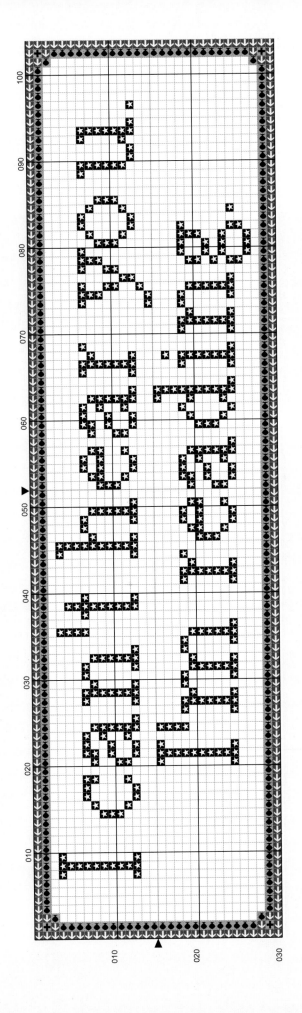

WE DON'T CALL THE COPS ☠SIGN☠

Supplies:

- 14-count Aida cloth
- Tapestry needle
- 10" x 10" Frame
- 6-strand floss

This colorful design advertises your indifference.

Design size:

140w x 140h stitches (10" x 10")

Instructions:

Following the general instructions on pages 09–10, cross-stitch in 2 strands according to the chart. Allow yourself a little extra fabric around the edges if you intend to frame your design. When all cross-stitching is done, mount the completed design in the 10" x 10" frame according to manufacturer's directions.

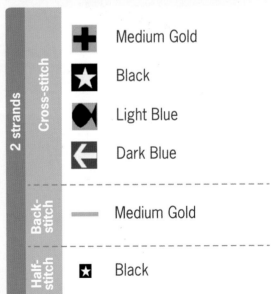

31

2 strands	**Cross-stitch**	✚	Medium Gold
		★	Black
		◆	Light Blue
		◀	Dark Blue
	Back-stitch	—	Medium Gold
	Half-stitch	★	Black

I SCOFF BECAUSE I JUDGE SIGN

Supplies:

- 14-count Aida cloth
- Tapestry needle
- 10" x 10" Frame
- 6-strand floss

This blunt sign lets everyone know what you really think.

Design size:

140w x 140h stitches (10" x 10")

Instructions:

Following the general instructions on pages 09–10, cross-stitch in 2 strands according to the chart. Allow yourself a little extra fabric around the edges if you intend to frame your design. When all cross-stitching is done, mount the completed design in the 10" x 10" frame according to manufacturer's directions.

	2 strands Cross-stitch	
✚		Medium Gold
ⵔ		Grey
◖		Light Blue
⬅		Dark Blue
◇		Dark Green
▢		Light Green
▽		Medium Tan

THE GIFT EVERYONE WANTS: SILENCE SIGN

THE GIFT
EVERYONE
WANTS:
SILENCE

Supplies:

- 14-count Aida cloth
- Tapestry needle
- 8" x 10" Frame
- 6-strand floss

This framed sign will bring peace into every household.

2 strands	Cross-stitch	▲	Bright Red
		★	Black
Half-stitch		◣	Bright Red
		☆	Black

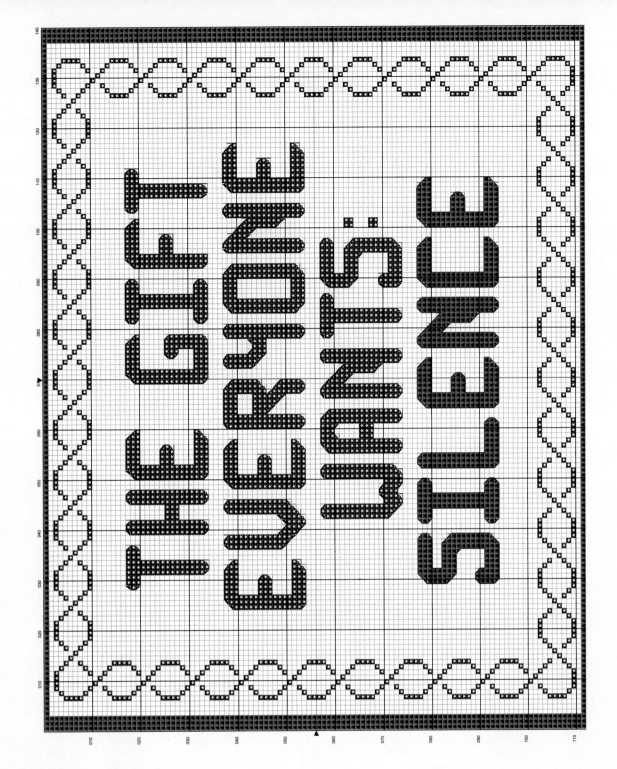

Design size:

140w x 112h stitches (10" x 8")

Instructions:

Following the general instructions on pages 09–10, cross-stitch in 2 strands according to the chart. When all cross-stitching is complete, mount in 10" x 8" frame following manufacturer's directions.

I'M MARRIED AND I LIVE WITH MY MISTAKES ☠ SIGN ☠

2 strands	**Cross-stitch**	✚	Medium Gold
		★	Black
		◆	Light Blue
		◄	Dark Blue
		▲	Bright Red
	Half-stitch	★	Black
		▲	Bright Red
		✚	Medium Gold
		◆	Light Blue
		◄	Dark Blue

Supplies:

- 14-count Aida cloth
- Tapestry needle
- 10" x 8" Frame
- 6-strand floss

This framed sign is a gentle reminder to not repeat the past.

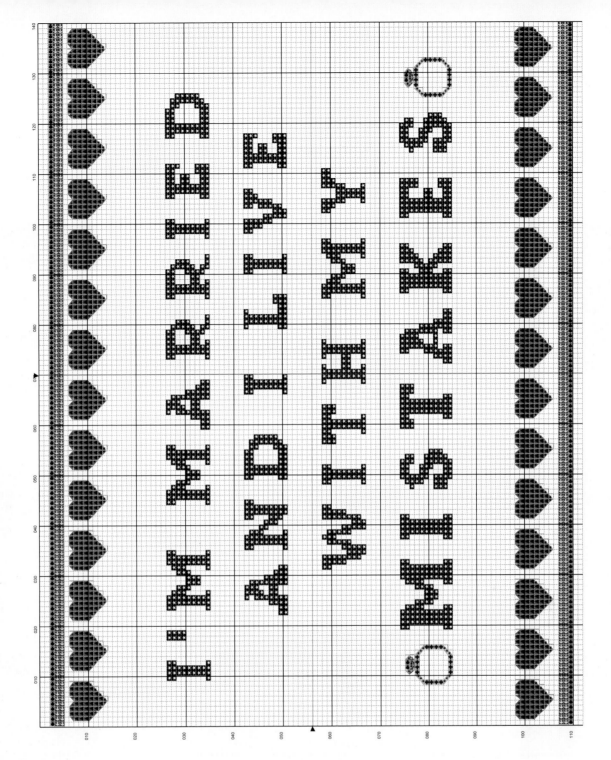

Design size:

140w x 112h stitches (10" x 8")

Instructions:

Following the general instructions on pages 09–10, cross-stitch in 2 strands according to the chart. When all cross-stitching is complete, mount in 10" x 8" frame following the manufacturer's directions.

I COULD ANSWER YOU, BUT I WON'T ☠SIGN☠

This sign lets everyone know when you've had it up to here with them.

Supplies:

- 14-count Aida cloth
- Tapestry needle
- 10" x 10" Frame
- 6-strand floss

2 strands Cross-stitch

○	Grey
▲	Bright Red

Design size:

140w x 140h stitches (10" x 10")

Instructions:

Following the general instructions on pages 09–10, cross-stitch in 2 strands according to the chart. Allow yourself a little extra fabric around the edges if you intend to frame your design. When all cross-stitching is done, mount the completed design in the 10" x 10" frame according to manufacturer's directions.

Tip: Self-adhesive mounting boards are an easy way to mount cross-stitched designs for framing. The boards have a pressure sensitive self-adhesive surface on one side for mounting your cross-stitch. Simply peel away the paper liner, center the design, and press firmly to adhere. You can purchase self-adhesive mounting boards in standard frame sizes, or cut to fit any size or shape.

CHEW WITH YOUR MOUTH CLOSED
☠ BIB ☠

It's never too soon to learn table manners.

Design size:

115w x 29h stitches (8.2" x 2.1")

Instructions:

Following the general instructions on pages 09–10, cross-stitch in 2 strands according to the chart.

Tip: We used a quilted bib with a 14-count Aida pocket measuring 8.25" x 4.75". The overall size of the bib is 9" x 9".

2 strands	Cross-stitch		
			Black
			Light Blue
			Dark Blue

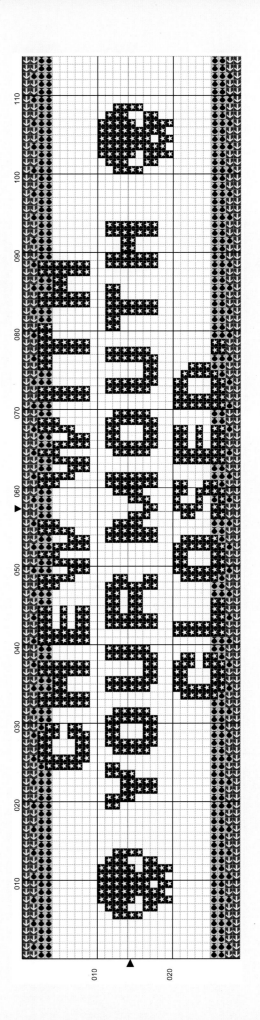

WASH YOUR HANDS
BEFORE YOU TOUCH ME
☠HAND TOWEL☠

This towel reminds your kids to stay clean when you're not around.

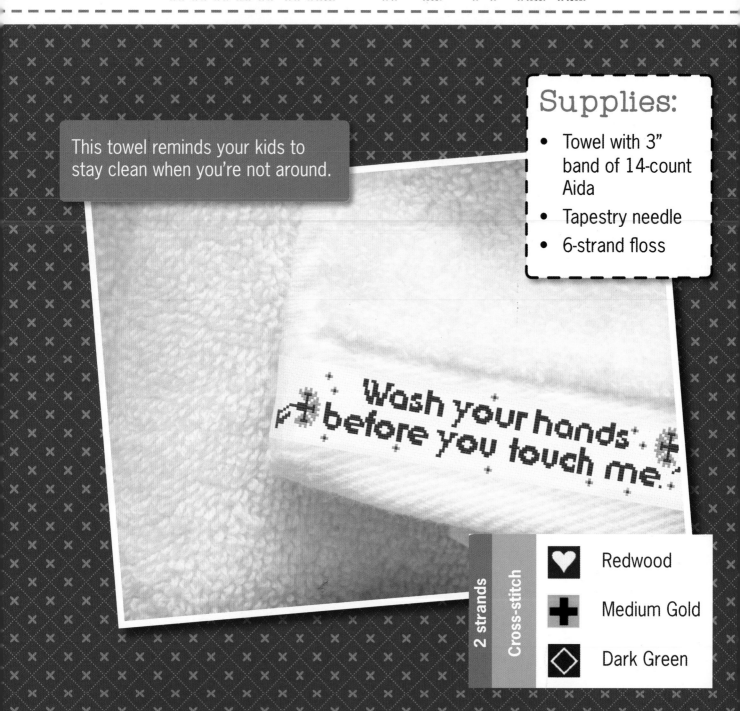

Supplies:

- Towel with 3" band of 14-count Aida
- Tapestry needle
- 6-strand floss

2 strands	**Cross-stitch**	♥	Redwood
		✚	Medium Gold
		◆	Dark Green

Design size:

115w x 29h stitches (8.2" x 2.1")

Instructions:

Following the general instructions on pages 09–10, cross-stitch in 2 strands according to the chart. Start stitching from the center and work outward. Follow the arrows on the sides of the chart to find the center of the design. Find the center of the Aida band by folding the towel in half lengthwise. Depending on the size of your towel, you can lengthen or shorten the border. If space allows, try adding more space between the words.

Tip: We used a white Huck towel with a 15" x 3" band of 14-count Aida woven in. The overall size of towel is 25" x 15". Try this pattern with other color combinations to match your kitchen or bathroom.

Care and Washing:

To clean your stitched towel, hand wash in lukewarm water with a mild liquid soap. Rinse in cold water. Lay flat to dry.

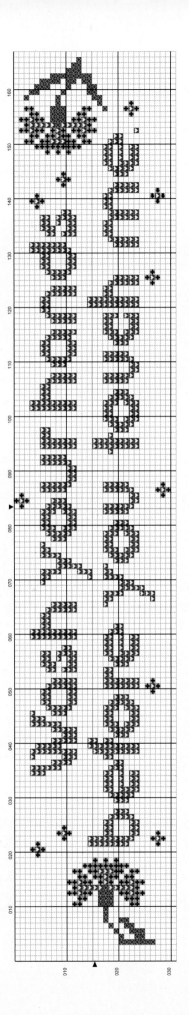

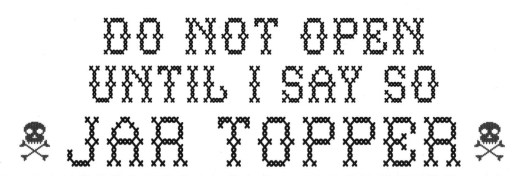

DO NOT OPEN UNTIL I SAY SO ☠ JAR TOPPER ☠

Nothing keeps those ravenous intruders out of your preserves better than this jar topper.

Supplies:

- Circular piece of 14-count Aida cloth with 2.75-inch diameter
- Tapestry needle
- Wide-mouth Mason jar with lid and band
- 6-strand floss

Design size:

32w x 33h stitches (2.3" x 2.4")

Instructions:

Following the general instructions on pages 09–10, stitch according to the chart.

When your cross-stitch design is complete, fill the jar with the desired contents. Cover the top of jar lid with your cross-stitched fabric. Place the covered jar lid on top of jar and secure with the outer band.

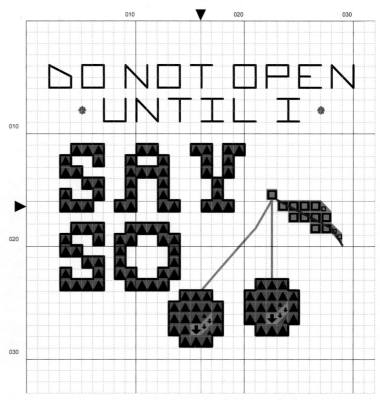

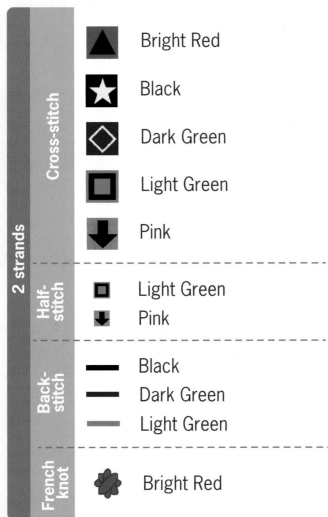

			Cross-stitch	
	▲	Bright Red		
	★	Black		
	◇	Dark Green		
	◻	Light Green		
	⬇	Pink		

Half-stitch
- ◻ Light Green
- ⬇ Pink

Back-stitch
- — Black
- — Dark Green
- — Light Green

French knot
- ❀ Bright Red

2 strands

NO I.D. NEEDED
☠ LUGGAGE TAG ☠

Travel in style with this cross-stitched luggage tag.

Supplies:

- 14-count Aida cloth
- Tapestry needle
- 3" x 2" rectangular keychain case
- White card for backing (optional)
- 6-strand floss

2 strands	**Cross-stitch**	★ Black
		◇ Dark Green
		▢ Light Green
	Back-stitch	— Light Green

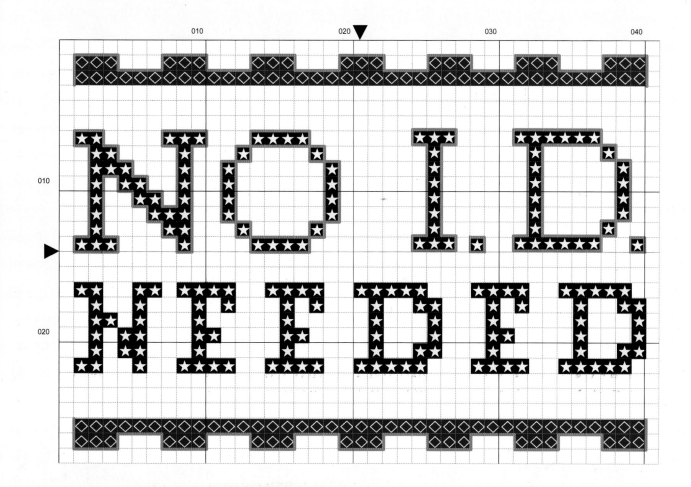

Design size:

41w x 28h stitches (2.93" x 2")

Instructions:

Following the general instructions on pages 09–10, cross-stitch in 2 strands according to the chart. When the cross-stitch design is complete, trim excess fabric around the edges until the design fits in the case. Snap the case shut and attach to luggage with a metal ring, a carabiner, a piece of string, or a plastic luggage tag loop.

Tip: If your case is visible from both sides, add your name and contact info to a piece of white cardstock for the reverse side. This will also hide the threads on the back side of your design.

Use this grid to chart your own design. Remember that one square in the grid represents one stitch on your Aida cloth.

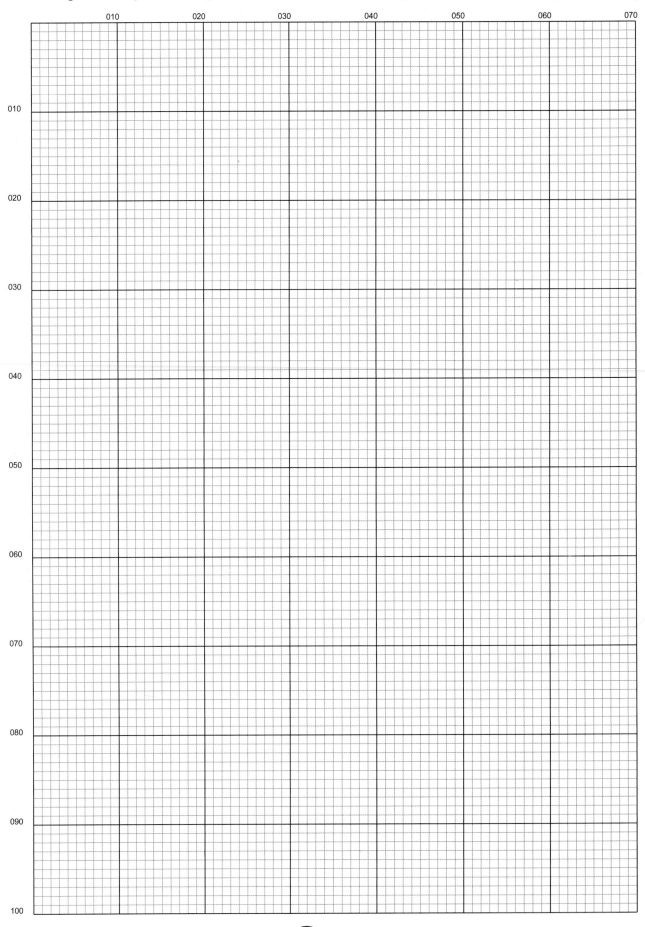